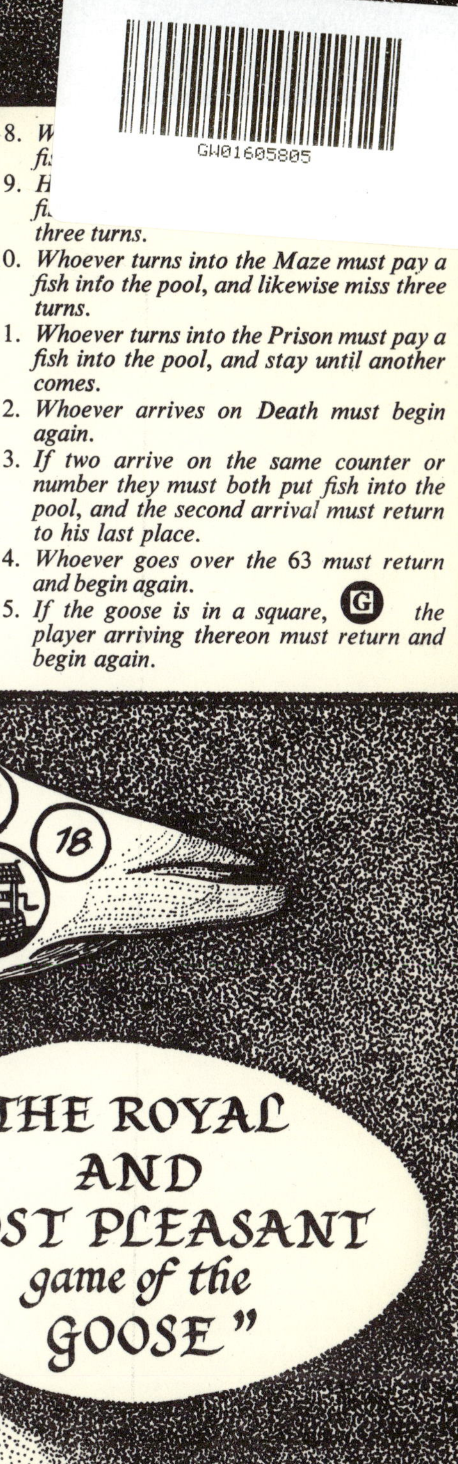

8. *W*
fi
9. *H*
fi
three turns.
10. *Whoever turns into the Maze must pay a fish into the pool, and likewise miss three turns.*
11. *Whoever turns into the Prison must pay a fish into the pool, and stay until another comes.*
12. *Whoever arrives on Death must begin again.*
13. *If two arrive on the same counter or number they must both put fish into the pool, and the second arrival must return to his last place.*
14. *Whoever goes over the 63 must return and begin again.*
15. *If the goose is in a square,* G *the player arriving thereon must return and begin again.*

QUINTILIAN

QUINTILIAN

WRITTEN AND ILLUSTRATED BY

JOHN HATFIELD

JONATHAN CAPE
THIRTY BEDFORD SQUARE
LONDON

FIRST PUBLISHED 1968

JONATHAN CAPE LTD
30 BEDFORD SQUARE, WC1
SBN 224 61344 8

PRINTED IN GREAT BRITAIN BY RICHARD CLAY
(THE CHAUCER PRESS) LTD.,
BUNGAY, SUFFOLK

Contents

For Marie and Paul

I

Where Oliver Explores, and Meets Quintilian

THE Black Swan was looking down at Oliver from his high pedestal. Oliver gazed back, and then moved two or three steps to one side and looked from there, away from the stare of those small dark eyes.

Perhaps he is more friendly if you know him, but he does look very proud, thought Oliver.

Walking back into the crowd of visitors looking round the museum he crossed the cobbled street, and stepped up on to the pavement. Oliver particularly liked all the quaint shops and buildings, never having seen such things in a museum before.

It's most unusual, he said to himself, to be walking past hansom cabs and fire stations and going round corners and crossing roads, without any fear of getting wet through in the rain or lost far away from home.

Turning to the Black Swan again, Oliver admired his beautiful crown.

But it seems to have slipped off his head, and all the way down his neck. Maybe it's too big for him to wear on his head, he thought. But I do like him. Him, and the tobacco boy, and William Tell with his floppy hat—and the tin soldiers and the acrobats. The policeman looked nice too, and the china dog with the bright eyes. Most of all the little dog. I shall try to find my way back to them all just once more today.

So Oliver set out with his most determined face, and threaded his way back into the secrets of the museum. The cobbles were difficult to walk on, and he had to go carefully, which was not at all easy when he was so anxious to find his favourites as quickly as possible.

Then there were corners that he had forgotten, and round them all there were so many shop windows to look in, filled with such strange and exciting things.

Thus it was quite by accident that he found himself looking at the buckles on the tobacco boy's shiny shoes.

Oliver's eyes travelled wonderingly up the little knee-length green socks that looked exactly like wool although they were made of wood.

Whatever has he got in that tiny box? His painted silver buttons look so real, and his white collar as soft as my softest scarf. He stepped back and bumped into the wheel of a stage coach, but the coachman didn't seem to notice, and the horse didn't jump at all.

But of course, horses filled with straw never move, thought Oliver sadly. Now, if I could sit in the coach and lean through the window I could see the tobacco boy's face properly. To his surprise a head suddenly appeared through the coach window and smiled at him. It disappeared, and then a fat man with a very red face looked out. Oliver realized that he could sit in the coach and lean out through the window, so he hurried round the straw horse and waited impatiently for the fat man to come down the metal steps.

And then he was inside himself and almost toppling out

THE
BLACK SWAN

again through the window as he leaned towards the tobacco boy. His mouth had been carved with a curious tight little smile, as though he really was trying very hard to talk, but didn't quite know how. His eyes were large and dark as pools, and he was holding out his little black box very eagerly. Oliver reached out his hand and took out a tiny scrap of paper, but it was nothing more than a ticket to the museum.

The coach rocked and Oliver saw that someone else was coming in. He smiled a quick goodbye to the tobacco boy and stepped down on to the cobbled street.

People are spoiling everything, he thought.

Oliver wandered off into a little snicket, with shops all round one side. He remembered that the acrobats, the tin soldiers and William Tell all lived together in one shop window.

I wonder if they get on well together, he said to himself. No doubt William Tell and the tin soldiers will be good friends. I think that the acrobats were above them on another shelf, and they looked very much bigger.

There it is. G. Pomfret. Toyman.

At first Oliver had the whole window to himself, and he knelt down to look at William Tell. He had a castle, straight up and down like a chimney, with tiny battlements and windows. The portcullis was drawn up, and there in the doorway stood a very small boy with an apple balanced on the top of his head. William Tell had a very determined expression on his face as he aimed his crossbow in the direction of his little boy. Oliver moved round and tried to squint along it, and he was almost sure that it was in fact aimed at the tiny apple, when lots of people rushed to the window and started to point and laugh at the acrobats.

Oliver supposed that this was on account of their faces, but their arms and legs were funny too, and their wooden bodies. They were painted gaily, and looked ready to spring about at any moment. Side by side they stood with legs braced and arms stretched upwards as they held on to a bar of wood. Oliver hoped that they were both taking equal shares of the weight. Or were they dangling from the bar? There was a wooden box behind them, with the lid open just enough to peep inside. He was surprised to see that it contained more arms and legs, painted with different patterns and colours. The writing on the box lid was nearly all far too small for him to read, but he could see the two big words ADMISSION FREE.

I don't see how anyone could ever get inside there – except the acrobats of course – even if it is free, murmured Oliver to himself. I suppose the tin soldiers could manage it, and William Tell. But I am not at all sure that William Tell could go anywhere without his castle, which would certainly stop him from getting in that box.

All this time more and more people were crowding round the window. With his mouth tightly closed Oliver talked to himself again.

They all say just the same things and pull the same faces. And the tin soldiers are very much smarter than any of them. So clever to stand still like that without having to stretch or scratch anything.

The red tunics looked as bright as they must have looked on the day they were painted. The black-and-silver muskets pointed forward or leaned neatly on the shoulders with no trouble at all. One soldier had fallen flat on his face. Perhaps from being in a battle, which was after all what he was for.

Oliver noticed to his delight that the shop was open, and he stepped eagerly through the door. There in front of him was the wax figure of Mr G. Pomfret. He really was a funny old man, very old, with his thin bent shoulders and his long bony nose with spectacles resting on the tip. He held a paint-brush in his hand, and the table at which he was seated was covered with half-painted wooden animals, lining up to sail on Noah's Ark.

They'll never manage in that ark, thought Oliver. Unless they keep on behaving as politely as they are now, and that is not very likely when the seas are rough and the ark begins to rock.

Mr Pomfret did not seem to be all that interested in camels and giraffes, and Oliver glanced quickly around his shop. The word MAGIC seemed to be written on an awful lot of things; boxes and packets and mysterious bundles.

I think that Mr Pomfret cares a great deal more for magic than monkeys, said Oliver, and Mr Pomfret's spectacles seemed to twitch on the end of his nose and shine just like the eyes of the little china dog. But this brief moment when Oliver almost spoke to the toyman was suddenly spoiled. More and more people had squashed into the shop behind him until there was scarcely room left to move. Oliver made up his mind that he would quickly seek out the little china dog, and that would have to do for now.

Then I shall know where all my favourites live and I can come back and see them some other time.

Oliver came out, and found himself having to move with the crowds, and quickly he realized that it was not at all the right way. He caught just a fleeting glimpse of the tobacco boy again, holding out his little box as urgently as ever.

Turning round he wriggled between two very squashy old ladies with large umbrellas on their arms, and then crossed the cobbled street, and back again past the toyman's most inviting door. He remembered that the china dog had been sitting in a window where one would not in the least expect to see him.

I think that it was all locks and keys, or was it locks and clocks? thought Oliver.

The dog's extraordinarily bright eyes and friendly face had so captivated him that he had not really taken much interest in the other things around him. The shop windows were almost all colourful enough to be remembered quite easily if anyone had particularly looked at them, but Oliver had not taken such care, and did not seem able to find his way.

Then the sight of a large lamp post made him think of night time when the museum would be closed, and everyone would have gone home.

After all, he said, I do live here *all* the time.

Oliver's father was the new curator of the museum, and they lived in rooms just a few corridors away from the very place where he was standing. After a moment or two, when his determination to come back that night had grown and grown, Oliver popped away through a door marked PRIVATE NO ADMITTANCE in very important-looking gold letters, much to the surprise of three or four people standing near by.

Oliver had found out long ago that to be seen yawning led to very definite steps being taken, and that night he wanted to be sure that they were taken quickly. So he yawned as many times as he could in full view of everyone, and it worked like magic.

With anxious looks and anxious talk about coming to new places, and trying to see too much at once, Oliver found himself in bed in no time at all. He knew that after about half an hour he could begin his adventure; until then he would ust have to wait in case anyone came to wish him a last good night.

When he heard a distant clock strike on the quarter for the third time he left his bed and dressed quickly. Closing his bedroom door behind him he crept along on the thick carpets and within a few moments he was down the last flight of steps, and opening the door on which were painted the very important-looking gold letters. Nobody was there to turn a head in surprise this time.

There was nothing to be heard except his own footsteps as he set out down the cobbled street, and everything looked very different. The shop windows had all been darkened, but the street lamps were lit, and the hansom cab and the policeman were just where he had remembered them. Almost straight away he went around first one corner, and then another that he had not been able to find in the bustle of the afternoon. With every step Oliver felt more and more certain that this was the right way, and when he passed a timbered post office next door to a saddler's shop he knew that the little china dog could not be far away.

The watch and clockmaker, is this the one? Another few steps, past the music shop, and there it was!

The locksmith's shop, of course!

And there was the beautiful little china dog, seated at the very centre of the window, looking straight into his face with the brightest eyes that Oliver had ever seen. As they stared at one another Oliver felt sure that there was something quite magical about this little dog, and he would not have been surprised to see him wag his curly tail, and jump down off his shelf in the window. Behind him the shop was deep in shadow, but when Oliver cupped his hands and pressed his face to the glass, he saw that in the shadows were hundreds of gleaming keys.

Just about all the keys and locks that ever were, he thought. Keys from the olden days when they needed so many, for locking away their secrets and their treasures.

Even the china dog had a gold chain shining amongst his curls, and a gold band round his neck, fastened by a heart-shaped locket. Oliver wondered if there could be a smaller lock in the shop, for this one looked smaller than a sixpence, and the keyhole was only just to be seen when he pressed his nose almost flat. The neckband was very delicately patterned with tiny shapes that looked almost like writing, and Oliver stared and stared before he realized with a start of sharp excitement that it was indeed writing – spidery little words written in an old-fashioned hand!

The china dog's eyes were shining brightly, and seemed to be urging Oliver to try as hard as he could, to try and read the mysterious message that he felt sure must be there. One by one he made out the words, saying them slowly to himself, making certain that he was reading them properly until at last he read them all aloud in a faint little voice that hardly sounded like his own:

QURIOUSLY SHAPED THE KEY,
WITHIN THE LOCK IT WAITS FOR ME.

The large curly letter "Q" did not seem to be right, but there was no doubt about the others, and Oliver read the two lines over to himself until he knew that he would never forget them. The fact that there was no key in the locket seemed almost impossible to him when at last he took his eyes away from the neckband.

"I know," he cried suddenly. "The shop! There must be keys for any kind of lock in there!"

Without wasting any more time Oliver pushed open the door and stepped inside, and as he closed it all the keys gleamed and tinkled. There were keys of every shape and size, hanging on hooks and dangling on chains, keys in caskets and keys on velvet cushions. Running his gaze around the crowded shelves Oliver saw fat keys and thin keys, warm copper-coloured keys and cold silvery keys. Quickly he moved around the shop, repeating the two lines over and over, and looking out for the smallest key of all. Without picking up a single key he knew that there was not one that would turn in the tiny locket.

I must go and look at the china dog again, he thought sensibly. Realizing to his delight that now he could go and pick him up and not have to strain through the thick glass, he hurried across to the shelving and pushed his hands through clusters of keys that rang like a chime of bells. He grasped the curly shape and lifted him into the shop.

Oliver sat down in a bright pool of light from one of the lamps outside and set the china dog down before him. He was hoping that somehow the key might have magically appeared in the locket, but it was not there. He picked him up and held him so close to his eyes that their noses touched. There was nothing to be seen.

Next he tried running his fingers along the gold chain, but it disappeared on the dog's back beneath one of his largest curls. Oliver ran his fingers back and up to the locket. Taking hold of it with his thumb and forefinger he pressed and poked; and then it happened like all the best surprises, when they are least expected.

The front of the locket sprang open, and there inside lay a tiny and most qurious key. Its rounded top was shaped in a curly letter "Q" exactly like the one on the neckband. It fell to the floor with the faintest tinkling sound, and shone in the lamplight. Oliver dropped on to it with a delighted cry, and closing the locket he popped the key into the keyhole and turned it with a click. For a moment nothing happened, but as Oliver watched breathlessly the china dog blinked first one and then the other of its glass eyes, wagged its tail, cleared its throat with a polite little bark, and spoke.

"I am Quintilian!"

"Oh," said Oliver, rising to his feet and then dropping back on to his knees. "I'm Oliver."

"I know that," said Quintilian. "The moment I saw you amongst all those people I said to myself, this is an Oliver if ever there was one!"

"Yes," said Oliver. "And I saw you, and I tried to find you again, but there were far too many people about."

"All that I could do was pop my eyes," said Quintilian. "Trying to let you know what sort of dog I am."

He began to jump about the shop, and Oliver watched with delight as all the keys shimmered and shook.

"And what sort of a dog is that?" asked Oliver.

"A very stiff dog at the moment," Quintilian replied. "Please excuse me leaping around like this, but I do get rather

stiff in the window. I must say, you found my key quickly enough. After all, there are so many keys in here, you might well have spent the whole night trying the tiny ones."

"Who did you have to turn the key for you before?" Oliver, who was beginning to feel dizzy watching Quintilian dash round the shop, was pleased to see that he had stopped running, and was busily arranging his curls.

"To tell you the truth," said Quintilian, "I cannot recall the last person to turn the key, but it must have been someone very much like you. It isn't anyone who could manage such a thing. Well! I suggest that we go out; everything will be different now you know. Turning my qurious key sets all manner of things off down here. And what a good night it is to be different. There's going to be a party; just the night for you to see everyone on their best behaviour."

Feeling that to be talking to Quintilian was the simplest thing in the world, Oliver opened the door and they stepped into the cobbled street.

Now the shop windows were all lit up, and he sensed a new excitement in the air; everything was completely changed.

"I think parties would be much better if people were not on their best behaviour," he said. "It spoils the fun."

"Well at least they start off like that," said Quintilian. "The fun comes later."

There came the unmistakable clatter of hooves, and turning round Oliver saw a hansom cab following them down the street.

"The guests must be arriving already," said Oliver. "Who could this be in the cab?"

"No doubt about that," replied Quintilian. "This will be

the apothecary. He always hires a cab because he likes to be the first to arrive."

"Will he be the first?" asked Oliver. "And where is the party?"

"It's not easy to say," yapped Quintilian. "Parties here tend to be all over the place, and then there is more room for the fun and games."

The cab stopped as Oliver and Quintilian turned to see if it was the apothecary. Oliver watched the occupant step out, an odd little man not much bigger than himself, wearing an embroidered waistcoat and a grey top-hat. His clothes were bulging as though all his pockets were full. In fact Oliver could see a bottle and some spoons sticking out of one of them.

"Ah, Quintilian," he said in a rather disappointed voice. "You got here first again. Or was it you? Were you here first?" Turning to Oliver he flourished a tin under his nose. "Have a medicinal lozenge! So good for excited children, then you can really enjoy the party!"

2

There is the Beginning of a Party ...

OLIVER thanked the apothecary and put the lozenge in his mouth. Judging by the noise there were plenty of guests approaching the place where they stood, and Oliver wondered if the party was going to start here, and then move on to all the different places.

A loud clattering noise was coming from around one corner, and the sound of running feet from another. Trying to guess which would arrive first, Oliver was delighted to see the tobacco boy appear, evidently in a great hurry.

"Take his message," said Quintilian to the apothecary. "I can never stop him from running all over me." And the apothecary raised his hand high in the air, not at all unlike a policeman. The other clattering noise seemed to be fading away again, and Oliver wondered who it could have been. He was glad at least that he would not have to take his eyes off the tobacco boy, who was offering his little black box to the apothecary. Quintilian was handed a small scrap of paper.

"The Black Swan is ready!" Quintilian turned and read the message to them both. As he read, the tobacco boy nodded his head in agreement, but he never said a word.

"No doubt you heard that," said the apothecary to Oliver.

"I hope that you both did," said Quintilian. "Well, this is the Black Swan's party, and when the most important person is ready it only means one thing."

"Quite so," said the apothecary. "At least one thing."

"Which is", said Quintilian, "that we must waste no more time here!"

"Is it the Black Swan's birthday?" said Oliver. "Is he the one up on the archway, with a crown around his neck?"

"Yes he is," said the apothecary. "Twice you are right!"

"He never said that," Quintilian yapped. "He never mentions birthdays. It is quite enough that the Black Swan said, 'There shall be a party in my honour.' I heard him say it myself."

"So did I." A very friendly voice spoke at Oliver's elbow. It was a white goose, wearing a dark-blue shawl. "In his honour. I was there at the time."

"Just because you were there makes no difference," said the apothecary. "I happen to remember that it is exactly one birthday since the last time the Black Swan gave a party, which would make it just about right."

They all started to walk briskly around the corner where the other noise had been, and Oliver hoped that they would find the noisy one.

"Why doesn't he wear the crown on top of his head?" He asked them all, but watched the tobacco boy particularly, hoping that he might hear him speak, but all the boy did was busy himself straightening his smart silk collar, handing Oliver the message box to hold.

"Safe keeping," said the goose, who was very talkative without a doubt. And she seemed to know all about the Black Swan, for both the apothecary and Quintilian agreed at once.

Oliver noticed that they were coming towards the toy shop, and that Mr Pomfret himself was standing in the doorway with William Tell and one of the tin soldiers.

"Heads are very unreliable things," explained the apothecary. "Why do you think people say 'muddle-headed' and 'dunderhead', and why do you think people are always shaking their heads when they don't know things? Besides, even their own hair falls off, and crowns are much more valuable than hair."

They all stopped to greet Mr Pomfret, and Oliver could see that William Tell had managed to leave his castle. He could see it in the window, and the little boy was sitting on the roof in his pyjamas eating the apple from the top of his head.

"What did I tell you," said the apothecary. "The apple has come off his head now. Fancy eating apples at bedtime! I must remember to give William Tell some of my special mixture."

"I suppose he is rather silly," Oliver replied, "but when you are not being allowed to go to the party, I should expect to do something nice, foolish or not."

Quintilian was talking loudly to Mr Pomfret all this time, who looked undecided about something, and was looking first at the clock on the opposite wall, and then back into his shop.

"Do you know what he's after?" said the goose, tugging at Oliver's sleeve with her beak. "He's after dressing up in his magician's robes – robes mind you – not common-or-garden clothes!" And the goose laughed knowingly to herself and winked at Oliver as though he knew just what she meant.

"I knew that he was very fond of magic," he replied.

"Fond of it!" The goose chuckled again. "It's all he ever thinks about. Dressing up and waving sticks about, and muttering words that nobody understands at all."

As they spoke the tobacco boy, who had disappeared mysteriously only two or three minutes before, came running up to Mr Pomfret's door. The toyman took the message out of his box and turned to one of the tin soldiers.

"Time to go and blow your bugle," he said. "The guard of honour have been gone ten minutes at least. No hope at all now for me to get into my robes! Run along now and we shall be right behind you!"

The tin soldier, who was in fact a bugler, saluted smartly and marched off. Quintilian smiled with his bright eyes and turned to Oliver.

"I know that I said that this party was everywhere, but just for a few moments it's going to be in one place, so that the Black Swan can make his speech."

Oliver thought very fleetingly that speeches could easily ruin a party, but then he realized that the sort of speeches that Black Swans with crowns would make may be rather different. Mr Pomfret closed his shop door and turned the key.

"I thought it wise to keep the acrobats in their box until the speechmaking is over," he said.

"Merciful," said the apothecary, applauding with his small hands.

"Wise, very wise," said Quintilian.

"Wise? I should say so!" quacked the goose. "The Black Swan finds them too much – A trial he called them once. A great trial, which is very serious."

They all set off in the direction of the archway. Lots of others apart from their little group were going too, and Oliver remarked to the apothecary that it was almost like ordinary daytime. Quintilian overheard and smilingly said that it was not at all like that, and after another look Oliver had to agree.

Two very small zebras from Noah's ark were walking along slowly in front of them, much to the annoyance of the apothecary.

"Ridiculous creatures," he said, "especially when their stripes are only half painted. And so slow. Shoo now! Shoo!" But the zebras only nudged one another and grinned at Oliver, and he knew that they did not worry in the least about him.

"Here we are," said Mr Pomfret at last. "What did I tell you? See, everyone is dressed in their very best finery. What a calamity to be the drabbest person here!"

Oliver was not expecting to see such a large gathering. There was a huge crowd, and the policeman was striding about importantly, doing his best to put people where they could see the proceedings. Quintilian laughed and said that it did not matter in the least, as the Black Swan was so high that everyone could see him.

"Not like trying to see something low!"

"There's nothing at all that is low about the Black Swan," said the goose. "He is the highest one of all in here!"

The tin soldiers jumped smartly to attention when they noticed Mr Pomfret, and one of them nudged the bugler. He stepped forward and tried to blow a fanfare, but seemed a little overawed, and could do no better than make a funny cracked noise. A lot of the audience would have liked to have giggled had the occasion not been so grand. Then Quintilian with a single bound jumped up on to a pillar box.

"Silence please!" he barked. "Silence now for the Black Swan!"

3

... *and Oliver makes an Awful Mistake*

AT first the Black Swan did nothing but preen his wings without saying a word. Then he inclined his head in a nod of thanks towards Quintilian, and reached up to his full height.

"I, the Black Swan, have no wish to keep you from your merrymaking, but would like to say a word or two, so that all of you – especially the little ones and the newcomers – will realize that even fun and games have good reasons behind them. The reason tonight is that yet another year has passed since I was presented with this beautiful golden crown by King Charles himself!"

The Black Swan thrust himself forward until the crown flashed in the light, and one of the zebras, who was just tip-toeing round the corner with his twin, stopped and covered up his eyes.

"I told you it was a birthday," whispered the apothecary proudly to Oliver.

"A crown birthday!" added the goose.

Both the apothecary and the goose had been able to say these things because everyone was clapping politely.

Then Quintilian told everyone to walk forward one by one, and put their gifts under the archway. For the first time Oliver felt a little alarmed, and his alarm grew and grew as he saw the numerous presents.

The first to step forward was the apothecary, who gave the remainder of his medicinal lozenges. William Tell produced an apple from under his cloak, and then a rag doll bowed daintily as she presented a large yellow duster.

"For polishing the crown," whispered Quintilian, and then vanished behind the crowd.

Next there was a large tin of metal-polish from the coppersmith.

"That's for polishing the crown as well," piped Noah's two ostriches as they walked forward with a bunch of white feathers under a little glass dome.

Then the coachman gave a coloured pencil, and Ebenezer Somebody-or-other gave a pearl-handled magnifying glass that he had had in his pawn shop for some time. The firemen had brought a silver bell, which they rang proudly, and lots of the smaller toys and animals cried "Fire! Fire!" and "Where? Where?" until they were told that it was just another present. The farmer gave a green cheese, and the innkeeper a punchbowl. There was a roll of coloured wallpaper from everybody at the doll's house, and a wineglass from the wine merchant. The policeman presented a whistle on a chain exactly like his own, and Mr Pomfret gave a conjuring set.

Oliver was beginning to wonder where Quintilian had gone when he appeared from around the corner with two kitchen boys, who wore tall white hats and chequered trousers. Everyone gasped as they saw the huge pink-and-white cake that they were carrying between them. On the top was a beautiful sugar crown.

"And everyone must eat a piece!" said Quintilian. "Goose! Would you be so kind as to cut the cake?"

Soon they were all eating, all, that is, except the Black

Swan who preened his wings once more before smiling generously down upon his guests.

Last of all with his present came the tobacco boy, running forward eagerly. He opened his black box and Quintilian took out the tiny piece of paper.

"HAPPY CROWN BIRTHDAY, that's what it says." And Quintilian turned round slowly, waving the paper so that everyone could see.

"They really have no idea what to give a swan," said the goose primly to Oliver. "I have given him a hand-mirror to see that his crown is straight. Or rather I will when this eating is finished. What have you brought?"

"That's just it," said Oliver, mumbling through his mouthful of cake. "I have nothing to give – you see I had no idea – "

"Of course you had no idea!" said the apothecary. "How could you? But you must admit that you knew enough about it to come! Coming here is all very well it seems, and being empty-handed doesn't matter apparently!"

Quintilian silenced the apothecary with the sharpest of barks.

"Oliver is going to recite a poem, silly! All schoolboys recite poems on occasions like this – when they have eaten their cake. Fancy you not knowing that!"

"This certainly calls for another fanfare," said Mr Pomfret, signalling to the bugler, who would not look his way at all. Oliver surprised himself by remembering at once that he did know a suitable poem for reciting to swans, because it was about a swan. Quickly saying the first line to himself to get it straight, he stepped forward to where the presents were heaped, and looked up at the Black Swan, who in turn looked down very attentively.

"I have no present," he said, "having only just got here this very evening. So I am going to recite a poem in your honour, very suitable for a swan."

Everyone went quiet, never before having heard a small boy recite a poem in honour of the Black Swan, or anyone else for that matter. Oliver held out a hand as casually as he could and began:

"Once I was as white as snow,
Across the waters I did go.
Now I am blacker than a crow."

He had to raise his voice slightly just before he got to the line about being black, because the bugler, having caught Mr Pomfret's eye at last, blew another very cracked noise on his bugle.

The Black Swan politely ignored this noise, as did everyone else, but he looked rather surprised, then very interested. Then he frowned.

Oliver looked at Quintilian, and supposed that he had better go on. He had an idea that maybe this was not the sort of poem to read in honour of the Black Swan, which was not helped by the apothecary's nervous cough.

"Crow, eh! Crows indeed!"

Oliver continued:

"Over the green fields I did fly,
Under a wide summer sky.
Now in a silver ... in a ... "

Oliver stopped and his ears turned a bright red. Now he knew for sure that it was the wrong sort of poem.

The Black Swan lifted his head gravely.

"Now in a silver *what*, may I inquire?"

"Dish," said Oliver flatly, feeling the goose step away from his side with a click-click of her tongue. "Now in a silver dish I lie."

There was an awesome "Oh!" from all around, and then a hush. With two little taps a pair of Noah's small sheep fainted right away. The Black Swan stiffened slowly until his head was so high that he looked higher than ever.

All his interest in Oliver and his poem, and the presents, indeed in the whole gathering, seemed to be slipping away.

"Really!" he said. "Now in a silver dish indeed!"

And he raised first one of his huge black wings and then the other. They spread out right into the shadows as he stretched up on his webbed feet. Then he folded back his head with a disdainful curl of his neck, and rose slowly into the air.

Everyone stared and stared and mouths fell open with gasp upon gasp. Within a moment the Black Swan had circled the whole gathering, and then, thrusting out his long neck in front of him, he disappeared over the rooftops.

4

The Party Ends with Some Solemn News

OLIVER made five wishes, one after the other. First he wished that he could run away and hide, and then better still, that he had never come to the party. This seemed a little extreme, so he wished that the Black Swan would come back, provided that he could wish that he had never recited his awful poem. Last of all he wished a sort of mixture, where the Black Swan was back, and he had not recited his poem, but that he had brought an acceptable present like all the others.

"I know just what you are thinking," said Quintilian. "Well don't! It doesn't matter really, because the Black Swan is very gracious when he stops and thinks about things. Come and enjoy the party! He'll soon be back, and he might have forgotten too!"

"Yes indeed," said Mr Pomfret. "What he needs is a bit of Pomfret party magic – and the acrobats, of course! I must go and let them out or goodness knows what they will be up to."

With that he hurried off towards his shop, closely followed by the bugler and William Tell.

"Now for it," said the apothecary. "The acrobats are very troublesome fellows!"

Before Oliver could guess what might happen next he saw that almost all of the crowd were busily rushing about, murmuring quietly, "Hunt the Button! Hunt the Button!"

They peered and poked into every corner, and under every ledge. They climbed lamp posts and scrambled up drainpipes.

"I hope it's a good big button," said Oliver to the goose, who was still being rather cool towards him.

"A poor game," she replied. "Only suitable for very small or very simple ones!"

Noah's animals seemed to have given up already and had started to play blind man's buff in a little wooden shelter, where there were seats for resting. Noah's wife had tied a spotted handkerchief round the eyes of a giraffe, and was busily turning him about.

"They all giggle and make far too much noise," said Oliver. "The secret is to stand very still."

"Not such a bad game," said the goose, trying to stretch her neck like the Black Swan. "But wait until you play *my* game – now that *is* a game!"

"Caught you!" shrieked the giraffe, as he grabbed at his twin. "It's the camel – one of the camels!"

How funny, thought Oliver. Whatever could it be but a giraffe with a neck as long as that? They don't seem to know much.

All the other animals were rolling about with laughter, and even the camel managed a thin smile.

A military band was assembling outside the fire establishment. They wore green tunics with white straps all over them, and shiny black hats and boots. But before they could make a single note of music there came a great clattering, pursued by the noise of running feet. It was the acrobats.

"So they were the cause of the funny noise," said Oliver to the policeman, who had stepped forward as though expecting trouble.

"The cause!" he said. "Most certainly *the* cause! A great deal of law and order is required when they come out! Now, now. Pray silence for the military band!"

The acrobats rocked to a stop for just a brief moment, and then one of them spun up on to the bar that they carried, and stayed there – upside down.

"Pray!" he shouted, loudly imitating the policeman.

"Silence!" shouted his partner, and then both together:

"For the MILITARY BAND!"

But instead of being silent they spun round and round, under and over the bar until nothing could be heard for the whirring and creaking of wood.

Noah's animals appeared to have forgotten about their game, and they all wandered over open-mouthed, leaving the giraffe clinging on to the nobbly corner of a seat.

"It's a monkey," he cried, "a monkey, I know!"

Oliver was surprised to see the policeman step backwards and smile sheepishly at the leader of the band, who looked very cross. The bandsmen put their instruments down on the cobbles and stared at the acrobats.

"Better let them get it off their chests," said the policeman. "After all it is a party. Plenty of time later for law and order!"

Mr Pomfret had arrived rather breathlessly on the scene. He was now dressed in a long blue gown, covered in moons and stars, and was carrying a pointed hat. Quintilian, who had been quietly eating a bowl of biscuits all this time, ran forward.

"Oliver," he said. "Mr Pomfret would appreciate it very much if you were not to guess who he is. Now that he has put on his robes he likes to be known as the magician!"

"Robes, I ask you!" said the goose. "Old curtains and card-

board! It takes more than curtains and cardboard to make a magician!"

The acrobats were now both standing on their heads, and kicking a large wooden button backwards and forwards to one another, as the magician slowly turned his pointed hat round, until the trailing white hair glued in the brim hung down his back instead of across his face. When this was quite in order he pointed his wand at the acrobats.

"Abracadabra!" he cried. "Acro and Bat!"

And the acrobats rocked to a standstill, as the button rolled to Oliver's feet.

"Now!" said the magician, as though this was the moment for which everyone was waiting. "Pomfret magic from the magician! If you will all be so good as to observe those two large wooden fellows – those noisy, loud, and unmistakable fellows – I shall endeavour to make them do something far more remarkable than spinning about, or kicking buttons up in the air. I shall, in short, make them *vanish* before your very eyes!"

"A likely tale," smirked the goose. "Now if only he would be quiet and let us play my game ... "

Oliver looked around with a smile on his face. He had no idea whether or not the magician was able to do such a thing. After all, some very unusual things were happening tonight. He saw that the poor giraffe was still clinging on to the seat saying all the names of all the animals from the ark. The rag doll had picked up the wooden button with a cry of delight, and was telling everyone that she had won the game. The magician was reaching to his full height and was waving his wand and counting in a louder and louder voice, " ... SEVEN, EIGHT, NINE ... " when to everyone's amazement the tobacco boy dashed round the corner and pushed his little box urgently right under Quintilian's nose.

The message fell out, and before Quintilian could grab it Oliver reached down and picked it up. He had an awful feeling about it, and sure enough, as Quintilian jumped up and down, he read:

THE BLACK SWAN HAS LOST HIS CROWN!

5

The Royal and Most Pleasant Game of the Goose

OLIVER handed the message to Quintilian. Except for the giraffe in the shelter everyone was standing quietly, just as they had when the Black Swan had flown away, but this time for much longer. The magician had stopped counting with his wand in the air; then Quintilian spoke.

"How careless of the Black Swan! That should teach him not to fly off in a huff!"

Oliver felt grateful to the little dog, but knew that it was rather more serious than that. Now things had gone from bad to worse. The goose would have turned white with alarm had she not been white already, and Oliver remembered how concerned she had been before.

The giraffe with the spotted handkerchief round his eyes was still struggling with the seat, and calling out the last few names he could think of.

"Porcupine?" he cried. "No. Sea-horse? Platypus?"

The acrobats whirled round towards the shelter.

"Pray!" said one.

"Silence!" said the other. And then together:

"For the matter of the Black Swan's crown!"

Noah nodded to them and gave his big stick to Oliver.

"Please take care of this for a moment or two," he said,

hurrying across to the giraffe, and scolding him gently as he untied the scarf. The apothecary was handing round his smelling salts, which were far too strong for most, and there was a lot of sneezing and weeping. The goose however took a deep sniff without turning a feather.

"Having shocks has never stopped me from knowing *exactly* what to do," she said, stepping out in front of the crowd, and reaching her neck high so that even the hedgehogs could see her.

"Pray silence!" shouted the acrobats together, leaping into the air, and clattering back on to their feet in a most effective way.

"We must play my game!" said the goose triumphantly.

"I knew it," sighed Mr Pomfret, peeling off his robes. "That beastly game. It takes so long!"

The goose ignored him.

"In that way everywhere will be searched, and the crown will be found."

Oliver was of course very puzzled, and was just going to ask Quintilian how on earth a game could be of any use, when he saw that everyone was hurrying over to the Fire Establishment. So he followed, side by side with the little dog.

"You'll see," he whispered to Oliver. "The goose *always* insists on playing her game when things go wrong. It's surprising how it settles everyone down."

"But what is *her* game?"

"Why, The Royal and Most Pleasant Game of the Goose!" cried the apothecary, who had evidently been listening to them.

Just past the Fire Establishment was a little house with a bow window, where the goose lived. Propped up inside the window Oliver could see a large board on which there was a picture of the goose, standing with her feet on the edge of a pool. There were circles and numbers drawn all over her.

The goose cleared her throat and spoke.

"Everyone must follow the rules, which I will explain once more so that there can be no mistake. You all know that I am really the prize for whoever wins the game, but as I have never been won before it's not very likely to happen tonight. Besides, the object is to find the crown!"

She then came hurrying round, handing everyone a small silver counter, and twelve red ones with the word "fish" on them in very small letters.

"These so-called fish are one of the reasons why nobody ever wins," said the apothecary to Oliver. "Once you lose all twelve you have to stay where you are."

"Can't move another single place," said Mr Pomfret.

It was then that Oliver noticed that some of the paving stones had numbers cut very delicately in their corners, starting of course at number one just by the goose's door, and winding away around the corner.

"Pass the two dice to one another in an orderly manner," said the goose, "and no squabbling. Everyone must shake a six to begin."

"This always causes a fuss," said Quintilian to Oliver, as they lined up to await their turn. "The first one to shake a six has got to put one fish in the pool straightaway."

"And just where is this pool?"

"The road is the pool. Just drop a fish down on to the cobbles."

"Do they ever cheat?" asked Oliver. He knew lots of people who were always cheating at other games.

"Not here," Quintilian replied. "I don't think they have ever heard of that, but they do some odd things that might look very much like it!"

Meanwhile the goose was watching the pair of dice go from one player to another without a six being shaken. Soon it was Oliver's turn, and, believe it or not, he shook a double six!

"Put one fish into the pool, please," honked the goose, "then off you go around the corner. This is your toll over the bridge, and you can go on to number twelve."

Oliver marched off excitedly to a thin wail of cheers. He was surprised to see a small bridge, with a pretty stone balustrade, in front of him and quickly hurried over it.

It seemed a great while before it was his turn again. Faint shouts drifted to his ears every few moments, but no one came to join him across the bridge. He guessed that there were no more sixes just yet. The goose eventually appeared just as he was becoming really impatient, and handed him the two dice.

"At least you'll get on," she said. "Have your next shake!"

"But why can't we all just get on without shaking dice?" said Oliver. "The crown would be found much more quickly then."

"That is definitely not allowed," replied the goose. "I always have lots of trouble getting people to follow the rules. Being a little boy I should have thought it much easier for you to understand."

"Well let's get on with it," said Oliver, shaking a one and a two, which seemed very few.

"Splendid!" cried the goose reassuringly. "You have a nice long way in front of you before the next awkward place—that is the well—I'll tell you about that when you get a little nearer." And she disappeared busily.

Counting his three places brought Oliver on to number fifteen. He noticed a small goose carved on number fourteen as he passed by. Next time round there must have been at least three or four new starters, for Oliver heard quite a crowd arrive at the other side of the bridge. He wished that he could see them.

No doubt someone will be catching up with me sooner or later, he thought. I do hope that they are all remembering to look for the crown, and not getting carried away with the game!

He was standing outside a costume shop, its windows filled with gowns of red and green, purple and blue, with white lace decorations all over them.

No need to look in there, he thought. Or *in* anywhere for that matter. If the Black Swan dropped his crown it must be outside, somewhere. And with dismay Oliver realized that it could be on a rooftop, or even down a chimney. Or perhaps down the well!

More shouting from over the bridge stopped his rather dismal train of thought. He heard the patter of feet coming over, and then to his surprise Quintilian appeared.

"So this is where you've got to," he said, jumping up and down.

"Yes, and I got here by following the rules," Oliver replied. "How about you?"

"I don't bother to play at all," said Quintilian carelessly. "I just move around as I please, keeping my eye on things!"

"That seems a good idea to me," said Oliver. "But tonight

we are supposed to be hunting for the crown. Why can't I run about with you?"

Quintilian was just beginning to look very mischievous, when he noticed that the goose was approaching again. She ignored him completely and handed the two dice to Oliver.

"Shake the dice," she said. "Off you go again!"

Oliver shook, and all he got were two ones.

"Hardly worth bothering about," he said, moving on two places. All he found there was a horse trough.

Quintilian ran up to it with him, and he and Oliver peered down into the dark water.

"Just the place for a lost thing," said Oliver.

Their faces peeped back at them, but there was nothing else. And then Oliver saw a very strange dark shape move over the water.

"Whatever was that? Did you see it!"

"It's the Black Swan!" said Quintilian excitedly. "Up there in the sky!"

Oliver was just in time to see the rather sad shape of the Black Swan moving away behind the rooftops and chimneys.

"Do you suppose he's searching?" he asked Quintilian. The little dog shook his head and his tail, both at once.

"Not he. He'll be going back to sit on his pedestal, and be all gloomy and thoughtful about things. He doesn't like to fly at night."

"Then he should never have flown off in the first place," said Oliver.

But then he remembered about the crow and the silver dish, and he could quite see why the Black Swan had flown away.

There was a sudden loud squawk from behind them.

There, only two or three yards away, stood a large white peacock, his tail fanned out around him.

"I'm the proud peacock!" it said. "I shall soon find the crown with my hundred eyes!" And the eyes of the tail seemed to stare past them into all the dark corners.

"You must have shaken lots of sixes," said Oliver. "I haven't seen you before."

"Hardly," said the proud peacock. "You are still ahead of me, and you haven't shaken very many! It really is not necessary – *not* that I don't intend to shake plenty of them very soon." With that the proud peacock decided to say no more, and just stood there with its tail swaying gently.

Before Oliver got his next turn there were quite a few more arrivals. The rag doll landed right on a square goose-stone, and with a sad little murmur disappeared back the way she had come. Then came John Peel on his grey mare, who was really far too small to carry such a large fellow.

"Tally ho!" he called. "Hunt the crown – great sport!"

Two camels arrived next, and then William Tell landed on the same stone. There was such a crush, and Quintilian laughed loudly.

"Back you go to your last place," he said, imitating the goose. The camels grunted with evident self-satisfaction, and closed their eyes smugly.

"No need to say who was *last*," said one of them.

"William!" cried Oliver. "Move back one place, or you will be wasted!"

"Cheating!" said Quintilian merrily. "I shall be on my way!"

"It is *not* cheating," said Oliver. "We are trying to find the crown, and if everyone keeps going backwards it will never be found. And if you must run off, please go the right way, and not back towards the beginning." Quintilian was half-way around the next corner.

"I'm going to the tavern," he shouted. "The taverner will be getting ready for us all, without a doubt."

"To the tavern!" cried John Peel. "That's the place for a stirrup cup!"

Evidently John Peel didn't worry about the rules either, and lots of the others seemed to like the idea of having a drink.

Oliver started to explain about the rules as almost all the players set off behind John Peel and his grey mare.

"Yes, yes," nodded the two tortoises from Noah's ark. "Let's see if we can get there before John Peel!" The proud peacock puffed out his feathers with rage, and shook his tail.

"Come back!" he screamed. "What about the rules?"

"Rules were made to be broken," said one of the tortoises. Then he turned to Oliver, who could only stand there in surprise. "I know that because I am one hundred years old."

Oliver knew then that if nobody else was bothered about the rules there was little point in him worrying about them, but he did feel a little anxious about what to say when the goose came round again. With one last look at the proud peacock, who was trying to catch sight of himself in the gown-shop window, Oliver walked off.

But I will try to count my steps on the stones, he thought to himself, and then try to get as many as possible when I have my shakes.

Round the next corner there was a music shop. The bugler was standing at the window, gazing lovingly at all the shining trumpets.

However did he get *there*? thought Oliver. I never saw him come past me.

"Ah!" said the bugler, jumping smartly to attention and saluting Oliver. "I was just about to muster a search party for you!"

"It didn't look much like that to me," Oliver replied. "And why did you want to find me?"

"To get the hedgehogs out of the well!" The bugler straightened his tunic, and stamped his feet just like a real soldier.

"I suppose that is the well that the goose told me about," said Oliver.

"I don't know about that," said the bugler. "But it is the well that the hedgehogs have fallen down, so I suppose that someone should have warned you about it."

"Someone should have warned the hedgehogs too," said Oliver.

"They know all about it," said the bugler. "Besides, it was worthwhile, because they have found the crown."

"Really?" cried Oliver. "What good news! But are they all right?"

"Hedgehogs roll themselves up into a ball when things go wrong," said the bugler. "So I expect they will be all right. Let's go and see!"

They hurried on past a candle and tallow shop and a penny bank. Then there was a doctor's house (which could be very helpful, thought Oliver) and an architect's house (which would be no use at all).

Quintilian appeared, but before Oliver could say a word about the crown or the hedgehogs there was a loud cry, and after quite a long silence a distant splashing sound. So many people were standing around that the well was only just visible in the courtyard of the architect's house.

"There goes the spotted pig!" they all shouted, as Quintilian looked at Oliver.

"I hope he doesn't land on the hedgehogs!"

"*Or* on the crown!" said the bugler.

"It was not the crown," said Quintilian, and Oliver felt very sad. "It was only orange peel – the hedgehogs refuse to believe it. They are just sitting in the water waiting for the bucket."

"That's an uncommonly good idea," said the bugler. "That's it! All we need is the bucket!"

"I keep trying to tell them that," said Quintilian. "But they will not listen, or mind out of the way."

"Now! Now!" came two loud voices behind them.

"Now! Now! What's going on here!" The acrobats came careering around the corner, and then stopped some distance from the well.

"Nine!" shouted one.

"Teen!" shouted the other.

"Double six we got!" And they spun round and round.

Somebody is keeping to the rules, thought Oliver. Somebody else besides the proud peacock.

"Rules," shouted one Acrobat.

"Are rules!" shouted the other.

"WE KNOW THAT!"

Meanwhile John Peel must have heard the advice about the bucket, for he had dismounted and was turning a handle that made loud squeaks and groans. Oliver heard a bump, and then a cheer.

"That will be the spotted pig," said Quintilian. "He always thinks of himself first."

There was a great deal more squeaking and groaning. John Peel was complaining of his aches and pains, but he kept on turning and at last the head of the spotted pig appeared.

"Steady now, steady," said John Peel. "Help the poor fellow out!" And the spotted pig was half lifted and half tipped on to the cobbles. To everyone's surprise two more small wet things rolled out as the bucket was tipped up.

"I put them in first!" said the spotted pig. "Before I got in myself," he added proudly. "And I ate the orange peel so that no one else can mistake it for the crown."

"To the tavern!" shouted John Peel at the top of his voice. "A stirrup cup to warm up the spotted pig! Finest thing there is!"

Within just a few moments the courtyard was deserted. The sound of John Peel's hunting horn and the clatter of feet faded away in the distance. As the goose came ruefully around the corner, carrying two large dice, a small wet hedgehog uncurled at her feet, and then another.

"You were right about the well!" one of them said to the goose. "It's very deep and very wet—and full of orange peel."

6

The Maze – and the End of the Game

OLIVER was far too warm in the tavern, so he decided to go outside and cool off. At one side there was a small garden with wooden seats, and tubs of sunflowers, so he sat down with his barley water and listened to the noise from inside.

They really are forgetful, he thought. First they forget about the crown, and now about the game. I can't understand where the goose has got to, she would soon remind them – unless she's forgotten too.

Then he heard another sound besides all the laughing and shouting. There were five or six sneezes, one after the other, and then the sound of noses being blown, followed by more and more sneezes. The voice of the goose made Oliver put down his barley water, and he peered between the sunflowers. Coming towards the tavern he saw the goose with the two hedgehogs, one of whom was blowing his nose into an embroidered handkerchief.

"Noah will send you two straight to bed I should think," said the goose. "If you can be trusted to go back without any further mishaps, that is."

"Someone must take us," said one hedgehog. "It's much too far to go by ourselves."

"I have no doubt that Mr Noah will take you himself," replied the goose. "He never has cared very much for my game – looking after you is all he thinks about."

Oliver was curious to see how the goose would set about things now, so he kept very still on his seat and watched.

"I should find them *all* in here with a bit of luck," she said, and without wasting any more time she disappeared into the tavern, leaving the hedgehogs looking wonderingly at each other. Inside everything went quiet, and then the hedgehogs suddenly rolled themselves up, and bounced as quickly as they could off the ends of the doorstep.

All the players came rushing out, some looking very guilty, some with smiling faces, some with bags full of pop-corn, some carrying bottles of ginger beer. They crowded together along the footpath, and Oliver decided to join them before the goose noticed him behind the sunflowers. She was trying to count them all, but it was very difficult for her, as there was lots of shuffling about.

"We all know that the tavern is *part* of the game, but it is no more than that! I know very well that you did not all get into there by shakes of the dice – see, I have them here!" And she lifted them up for all to see. "Mr Noah will be taking his hedgehogs back, and some of you will have to stay at the tavern and miss three shakes – that *is* one of the rules!" With that John Peel and the apothecary excused themselves politely and went back inside. "No more nonsense," continued the goose. "You can all start again from the pillar box here, it's just next to number thirty-three."

After a few hiccups and beg-your-pardons the dice-shaking started again. Off went William Tell, followed by the bugler, the camels, and then the acrobats, who were surprisingly quiet.

"They can't spin round just yet," explained Mr Pomfret as Oliver had his shake. "They swallowed their bitter lemons far too quickly." Quintilian appeared from nowhere as Oliver went on his way.

"I'll count for you", he said, bouncing up and down, "and see that you keep on the right number this time!"

When he called for Oliver to stop, he found himself with his nose pressing up against a yellow wooden door. It was just like being at the locksmith's window except that he could not see through, and Oliver wondered what might lie behind here.

"THE MAZE," he read out aloud. "Do we go straight in?"

"Of course," said Quintilian. "Turn the handle!"

With a loud creaking noise the door opened and they tumbled through.

"I know what mazes are," said Oliver, "rows and rows of hedges where people get lost looking for the way out!"

"It could be where the crown got lost," said Quintilian. "It's very big, and wide open from above."

There was a bright moon shining that Oliver could not remember seeing before. It made the hedges of the maze look a dark-blue colour, with silvery lines round them, and it was just as warm as it had been in the tavern. Oliver thought that he could smell roses. He quickly lost all sense of direction, and the moon was popping up and disappearing again every time they rounded a new corner. He thought it might be useful to find a star to follow, but there were so many he decided not to bother.

"Let's just go on round all the corners," he said to Quintilian. "One way is as good as another in a maze. It might be easier if we forget about trying, and get on with the search, of course."

There were already several others in the maze. Some

seemed to be going their way, but it was hard to tell, and Oliver certainly met lots of them more than once. Taking another turning he was surprised to find a fountain, its water tinkling and silvery in the moonlight. William Tell was sitting with his feet in the water, and the bugler was using his bugle as a drinking cup. He usually managed to get a few drops before all the water poured out of the mouthpiece.

Quintilian told Oliver that this maze was quite different from others, and to show him what he meant he took him round the next corner. There were all sorts of fruit trees growing up against the dark hedges, covered with orange and yellow fruit.

"It looks to me as though you know your way about in here," said Oliver, picking himself a large yellow apple. "Do you happen to know the way out all the time?"

"That's not important!" said Quintilian. "You keep on telling me that we are looking for the crown, and it could be anywhere. In here the important thing is to keep awake. Falling asleep is the main reason why most of them will have to be carried out of here."

"And who carries them out?" asked Oliver, yawning.

"The giraffes of course," said Quintilian. "Their necks are long enough to see over the tops of the hedges!"

Oliver noticed that there were lots of people and animals fast asleep on the soft grass. The two dappled ponies were dozing away on their feet, propping one another up. He also saw the spotted pig and the rag doll, who must have decided not to go back to the start after all.

"They must be tired," Oliver whispered. "So am I, quite tired anyway." He popped the apple up to his mouth so that Quintilian would not see him yawning.

Lots of small coloured birds were darting about, piping shrilly, and the noise seemed to make him feel more and more dreamy. He hoped that the giraffes would come soon, as all sorts of sleepy scents and perfumes were drifting to him.

As they turned another corner Oliver thought that he had found a new fountain, but when he saw the bugler standing there, and then William Tell who was now fast asleep with his feet still in the water, he knew that it was the same one.

"This maze is most amazing," he said, and turning to the bugler he asked him how it was that he was still wide awake.

"Sentry duty," he replied. "Lookout for the giraffes."

"In that case I can have a little rest," said Oliver.

He was just settling down comfortably at the side of the curly-horned sheep when there was a funny wet blast on the bugle, spraying water all around.

"Here they come!" shouted the bugler. "The giraffes are here!"

To begin with Oliver thought that two long poles were wobbling about in the distance, but as they came nearer he saw that the bugler was quite right. It was the giraffes. Already they had lots of small people and animals clinging round their necks, and they were swaying about in the moonlight, first coming near and then going away.

Oliver told the bugler to blow again, as William Tell was still fast asleep.

"And then they'll know where we are," he added.

Next time the bugler managed a really good blow. Oliver was only just in time to stop William Tell from falling into the water, and the dappled ponies jumped right off their feet. The spotted pig sat up with a jerk, and the rag doll was asking Oliver where she was as she turned round and round rubbing her eyes. Quintilian told them that they must not fall asleep again as the giraffes would not be able to carry anyone else by the time they got to the fountain.

"How will they ever know that everyone has been found?" asked Oliver.

"They won't," replied Quintilian. "They will manage *most* of the players, and the policeman finds the rest. He knows his way right through the maze, and he takes waifs and strays to the prison."

"Prison!" said Oliver. "That doesn't sound at all nice to me."

"It's only part of the game," said Quintilian. "The policeman takes them there for company, and they all have a jolly time together." Oliver looked at the little dog.

"If the policeman knows his way around so well he might have come into here in the first place, and searched thoroughly for the crown. But I suppose that would not be part of the game."

The long necks of the giraffes suddenly appeared over the hedge.

"Aha!" said one to the other. "There are usually more than this at the fountain."

"This way," said the other. "No more room for passengers. Just follow us!"

The rag doll took hold of one of the giraffes' tails, and William Tell held her other hand. The bugler insisted on walking at the very back.

"As a sort of rearguard," he explained.

The giraffes stopped at almost every turn, and reached up as high as they could. Oliver laughed at this because all the little ones clinging round their long necks slid down, and the

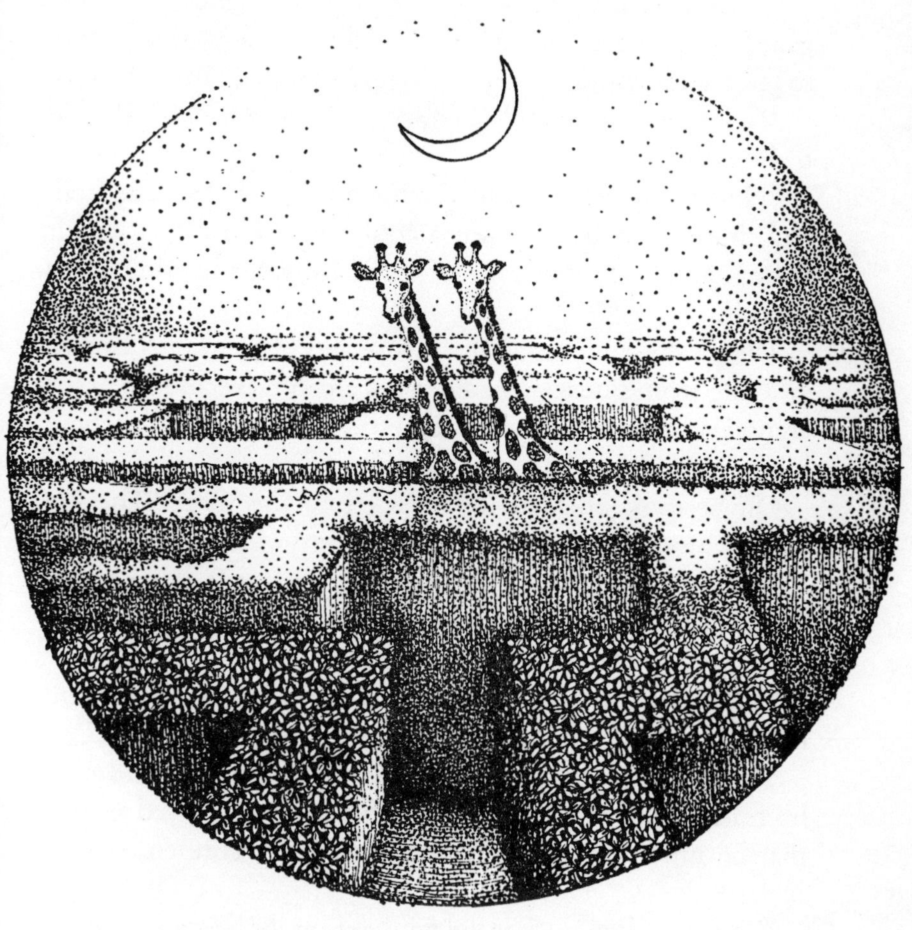

giraffes had to lower their heads and slide them back up again. And nobody even looked like waking up.

On and on they went. Sometimes the giraffes stood and gazed for so long that Oliver thought that they were going to fall asleep, and that everyone would finish up in the prison.

"Not that there could possibly be enough room," he said to himself.

"Nearly out now," said Quintilian. "I can feel the fresh air." Sure enough there was a cool breeze blowing towards them, and all the perfumes of the maze went wafting away with it.

The giraffes quickened their pace, and Oliver saw a lantern swaying from side to side. The policeman was standing in the archway of the yellow door, and the goose stood just behind him.

Oliver took one last look back into the maze. The big yellow moon was settling down on top of the hedges, and only the faint piping of the coloured birds was to be heard. The policeman was counting all the players, and writing in his large black notebook.

"Now for the stragglers," he said at last, and off he went through the yellow door with his lantern.

The proud peacock was standing a few feet away preening his feathers and looking very haughty. Oliver guessed at once that he must have done something clever. Sure enough he had.

"The proud peacock is the winner tonight," said the goose. "Not that he got to the end, but he did far better than anyone else."

The proud peacock stared at them all for a long time before he spoke.

"I happened to run out of fishes. I got to number fifty-seven! A number that I do not recall ever being reached before."

"But did you find the crown?" said Oliver, who was not at all impressed.

"The crown? Dear me, no," replied the proud peacock. "Nowhere to be seen. Nowhere."

Everyone looked ready for bed, and Oliver realized how sleepy he was. Then came a strange clicking and whirring over their heads. There was a large gilt clock on a near-by shop, and two tiny doors had opened at either side of the face. Two little men dressed as flunkeys approached one another in the clock centre, and bowed. One carried a gong and the other lifted a hammer above his powdered wig, and then brought it down on the gong: once ... twice ... three times ... four times ... They bowed again and marched back through their respective doors.

"Four o' clock!" said Oliver. "It can't be!"

"Time to go!" said Quintilian. "The dawn will soon be here—off we go!"

And he bounded away through a narrow alley with Oliver close behind. After a few twists and turns they came to a breathless halt in front of the dark-blue door marked PRIVATE NO ADMITTANCE.

"There you are!" said Quintilian, puffing and blowing. "Bed for you, shop window for me. And don't forget to come back soon—we still have the crown to find!"

In a flash the little dog was gone, and Oliver opened the door. Without waiting for the creaky stairs to quieten down he sped back to his bedroom with his head in a whirl.

7

Powdered Horn of Unicorn

OLIVER thought that the next night would never come. It took so long that there was plenty of time to get over feeling tired.

After all, he said to himself when at last he slipped through the blue door, I did have a short sleep in the maze!

Within a few moments he was turning the key in the locket around Quintilian's neck. The little dog bounced about, pleased to see Oliver again so soon.

"Has the crown been found?" asked Oliver, twisting round and round as Quintilian raced around the shop floor.

"Found?" he replied, tumbling over like a clown. "Dear me, no! Nothing will have happened since you went back to bed. I just had to give everyone time to get home before I sat in my window – then the time just stands still until I start off again! Nobody will have done or thought or found anything. I understand that the Black Swan is back on his pedestal, but that he is speaking to no one."

"I never thought he would sulk," said Oliver, as they walked out into the street. "Sulking never gets me anywhere, and I don't suppose it gets swans anywhere – black or white. Now I *have* been thinking, and there are two things I want to try.

"First of all, Mr Pomfret is a magician, and as this is a very magical sort of place we must see if *he* can get the crown back."

"Magician!" laughed Quintilian. "Mr Pomfret likes to think he is, just because his shop is full of wands and crystal balls, and big purple bottles. But I have never known him manage to turn a fly into a flea – never mind to conjure up a crown!"

"I should think no one has ever asked him to do it before, that's all," said Oliver. "Finding crowns may be quite easy to him."

"Then why do you suppose he never did it last night?" said the little dog.

"Magician's have this question of pride," said Oliver. "They do like to be asked, I'm sure. Now let's go and see him at once!"

When they arrived at the toyshop Mr Pomfret was busy washing spots of mud off the feet of Noah's animals. Mr Noah was watching anxiously, and telling him that the hedgehogs were in bed with bad colds. He went on to say that if a larger animal got its feet wet, a smaller animal like a hedgehog got everything wet.

"But they fell into the well," said Mr Pomfret. "If you go falling into wells what can you expect?"

Oliver excused himself for interrupting, but he had something very important to ask Mr Pomfret. The toyman looked pleased, and said that he was all ears.

"You *are* a magician as well as a toyman?" asked Oliver.

"You should say that I am a toyman as well as a magician," said Mr Pomfret. "Being a toyman is quite unimportant when one is indeed a magician like me!"

Mr Noah could see that he would have to finish cleaning up his own animals, for Mr Pomfret was already draping himself in the dark-blue robe. Then he put on his pointed hat covered in stars and moons, and turned to Oliver.

"There!" he said triumphantly. "Now who says that I am not a magician?"

"Good," said Oliver, "just as I thought. Now what I want you to do is to bring back the crown by magic!"

For a moment the magician (as he had now become) hesitated, but the sight of Quintilian shaking with mirth and one of the goats winking at Mr Noah was too much for him. Everyone began to gather round as he triumphantly produced an enormous leather-bound book from under the counter. The tin soldiers stood in a very straight line nudging one another with excitement, and the bugler prepared to blow on his bugle.

The magician stopped turning the pages and stabbed his finger down so hard that the dust flew out of his book.

"I have it!" he cried. "Why didn't I think of this before? All one needs is a little encouragement. Dear Oliver! How clever of you to think of me!"

And with a trembling voice he began to read from his book:

" 'For The Rightful Recovery Of Things Unaccountably Disappeared!

'REQUIREMENTS:

'1. Something similar in kind or colour to that which is to be recovered.' "

"Orange peel!" said William Tell. "Very similar – just you go and ask the hedgehogs!"

The magician nodded his agreement and sent the tobacco boy off with a little note in his box.

"That's that! Now:

'2. Something worn by the owner!' Easy! I have quill pens made from the Black Swan's feathers in this very shop! One of *those* should do!"

And after a rather frantic search the biggest and blackest of all the quills was put on the counter just as the tobacco boy ran back in clutching an orange.

" '3!' " said the magician. " 'Powdered horn of unicorn!' Hm ... Powdered Horn ... Yes—I have, I have!"

"He has, he has!" chanted the acrobats, leaping and spinning until everyone felt dizzy.

The magician was tearing open drawers and cupboards, packets and boxes, cases and bottles, throwing coloured string and paper over his head in a whirl of excitement.

" 'Powdered horn of crumpled cow—Powdered horn of white rhino ... ' No, no, no! Here it is—The powdered horn of a unicorn!"

He opened a small stone jar and blew into it gently, and there was a cloud of white powder that settled all over his spectacles. Oliver had peeled the orange and put the peel on the counter with the quill. The magician cleaned his spectacles and returned to his book:

"Cover one and two with a shawl
Then sprinkle the powder over all.
Close your eyes and count to three,
Open them, and you should see
A most rightful recovery!"

The magician grabbed at the shawl of the goose, who had said nothing all this time, maybe because her game had failed to recover the crown. Shaking with excitement he spread the shawl over the quill and the orange peel, and shook the fine white powder all over the shawl.

"Will everyone please close their eyes," cried the magician. "Listen to me counting, and when I say Three! everyone open them instantly!"

With a great deal of scuffling and giggling everyone covered their eyes with their hands and waited breathlessly as the Magician began to count:

"One ... Two ... THREE!"

8

Oliver Meets the Pedlar Doll and overhears something of Great Importance

ALL the heads bobbed up like corks, and every pair of eyes stared at the counter. There was a stunned silence, followed by a great outcry of voices, shouts of laughter, and gasps of astonishment.

The small powdery pile was still there, looking not one little bit different. Oliver thought for a moment that the magic might have worked after all, and he jumped forward and pulled the shawl up into the air with a flurry of Powdered Horn of Unicorn. Sneezing started all round the shop, and then hoot upon hoot of laughter broke out as the powder settled.

"One scraggy feather!" shouted one of the acrobats.

"And powdery pieces of orange peel!" shouted the other. "What magical magic!"

"Sir," said William Tell, turning to the magician, "you must have done something wrong ... " but his voice trailed away to a squeak.

Everyone turned to look where the magician had stood. Where had he gone? There was no robe, no pointed hat, no toyman. Just a pair of spectacles on the floor. Oliver was more surprised than he could ever remember. He turned to the watching crowd.

"He has vanished himself—that's what he's done!"

"He has, he has!" yelled the acrobats.

"He's done the disappearing trick!" And round and round they spun. The tin soldiers were turning the pieces of orange peel over and over, scratching their heads. Quintilian had laughed so much that he could hardly speak. The astonished face of the coachman was squashed against the toyshop window, and even his horse seemed to be staring with its mouth hanging open.

Oliver decided that it was time to try his second idea, and without wasting another moment he walked out of the shop, leaving the rest searching every nook and cranny, and chattering excitedly.

"What were all that?" asked the coachman, pushing his top hat to the back of his head.

"Just a bit of accidental magic," said Oliver. "Have you got room for one small passenger?"

"Passenger?" said the coachman. "Surely, surely, as long as you don't want to go anywhere particular. At first, that is."

"Oh, that's all right," said Oliver. "Nowhere particular—just as far around as possible."

"A sort of grand tour?" said the coachman. "I knows just what you means!" And with that he opened the door of his coach and helped Oliver up the small metal steps.

It was quite dark inside at first. Oliver could see that one side of the coach was filled with what looked like a lady, with two or three children sitting on both sides of her. He blinked and hoped that the lady would not mind him staring. Now he could see her small pink face, nodding kindly to him under the shadow of an enormous hat, covered with black lace and flowers and tiny birds. At first she didn't speak, and after smiling politely back at her Oliver turned to look at her children. Now he could see quite well, and there were more and more surprises waiting for him. There were no children at all! The lady's dark-red cloak fanned out from her shoulders and reached to both ends of the seat. On her knees was a huge wicker basket – the biggest that Oliver had ever seen, for it reached to both ends of the seat, just like the cloak.

As the lady nodded and smiled again there was a gentle tinkling sound, the rustling of silk, the tap-tap of wood upon metal, and the clink of glass. The only thing that Oliver could think of at first was a Christmas tree, for the lady was spilling over with all manner of trinkets and things. There were pots and pans, spoons and bottles, lanterns and toasting forks, socks and scissors.

"I do believe that you have never seen a pedlar doll before," she said at last, in the most musical voice that Oliver had ever heard. "I have to carry all these things with me, because I'm going to the market."

"I'm Oliver. I suppose that I must be going there too, in that case."

Oliver could not take his eyes off the contents of her basket. In fact the pedlar doll seemed to be covered in things, almost from head to foot. He saw parasols and ribbons, shoe-laces and bottles of scent, mending silks and bobbins, wax fruits and egg-timers. And as the pedlar doll laughed softly at his surprise everything shook and shone, nudged and clicked.

"I get around almost everywhere," she said, "but the market is the best place for me to sell my wares."

"I'm looking for a crown," said Oliver. "I don't suppose you happen to have seen one in your travels?"

Music
by
A Gran
March
TO

"A crown?" said the pedlar doll, straightening her beautiful hat. She reached down into her basket and turned over a pile of sheet music. "Phosphorous matches," she said, "smelling salts, white lace collars. No. A crown is one thing I haven't got. Do you mean a *real* crown?"

The coach was trundling down a narrow street that Oliver had never seen before. He noticed a barber's pole and a bookshop, then a butcher's shop, with the butcher standing in his doorway. The pedlar doll waited patiently for Oliver to finish looking, and then she asked him again.

"A real crown?"

"Oh, yes, sorry!" said Oliver. "It certainly is a real crown, it belongs to the Black Swan and he lost it, and it was really all my fault ... "

He was feeling quite tearful, and the pedlar doll gave him a large mauve sweet from her basket.

"Now I see," she said. "You mean *the* Black Swan. I know who you mean now. And that beautiful crown is lost? Well I never. Dear me."

"All I did was to say a poem," Oliver explained. "Six short lines and that was it."

"Do tell me," said the pedlar doll. "How very odd."

"Well," said Oliver, "it was only one short line that spoiled everything. Five of them were quite all right ... " he stopped again.

"Never mind that part now," said the pedlar doll. "I take it that something upset the Black Swan and he flew away?"

"How on earth did you know?" said Oliver, looking very surprised.

"It has been known to happen before," she replied. "But it

is the first time I have known him lose his crown! Of course, the important thing is to find it."

"Just what I am trying to do," interrupted Oliver. "I want to look around everywhere. Somebody is bound to know where it is, unless it dropped in a river or something."

The pedlar doll took out lots of pieces of blue and yellow ribbon, and sat fashioning them into bows and flowers.

"Look around and listen," she said. "Listening is often the best, and if you get out with me at the market you'll hear more gossip in five minutes than in a week anywhere else."

"Will you listen too?" asked Oliver. "If you don't mind?"

"I surely will," said the pedlar doll. "Two lots of ears are better than one."

She gave Oliver a black-and-white bull's-eye, and he sat without speaking as the pedlar doll tied her ribbons and the coach jogged along. In fact, before another word was spoken they arrived at the market cross. The coachman came round to open the door, and it took a very long time for the pedlar doll to get out. Not a thing was dropped.

"You be back here in half an hour mind," said the coachman to Oliver. "Then we can get on with our grand tour. You can't mistake the market cross wherever you are, it sticks right up in the air."

The pedlar doll smiled at the coachman and gave him a brown leather belt, which he straightaway strapped round his middle. Then he strode off lifting his top-hat to one and all.

"You go that way", she said to Oliver, pointing to the right, "and I shall go this way. And remember to listen as well as look." Oliver swallowed the last tiny piece of bull's-eye.

"I do hope I find the crown," he said, and with a wave he went on his way.

Just like when I was seeing everybody for the first time, he said to himself.

There were stalls in long colourful rows, selling almost anything you could want. There were cages of singing birds, oil-lamps and candles, fruits and flowers, kittens and codfish. There was a Punch and Judy show, and an organ-grinder with a dancing bear and a monkey to collect pennies in a hat.

Walking about with large shopping baskets there were ladies with silken bonnets and red-faced farmers, nannies wheeling tall prams, and clockwork soldiers in red and gold.

Oliver saw that all the soldiers had little gold crowns on their hats – almost like the Black Swan's crown – and for no better reason than that he started to walk along behind two of the very smartest ones. They were laughing and joking, and their silver spurs rang as they walked.

He could see the keys for winding them up in the middle of their backs. Every now and then they stopped to buy the sort of things that real soldiers buy, like metal-polish and boot blacking, tobacco, and pipe-clay. Oliver wondered where they came from, and watched as they stopped at a bric-a-brac stall. They picked up a small brass cannon and pretended to fire it, then a silver sword in a sheath, with rich silk sashes.

"Sell you one just like this," said one clockwork soldier to the stall keeper. "Better than this one, any old day."

"Sell you a crown!" said the other soldier. "Big as my hat and bright as sunlight!"

Oliver shrank into the sides of the canvas stall and listened with all his might.

2
FAMILY
BUTCHER

"Go on," said the first soldier. "A marvellous thing like that drops out of the sky, and you would sell it on a market stall!"

The stall keeper grinned at them both.

"Out of the sky, you say?"

"Like a shooting star!" said the first soldier. "Right on the sentry's rifle in the middle of the night."

Oliver nearly jumped in the air with excitement. He ran out and tugged at the scarlet tunics.

"You have got the crown!" he cried. "The Black Swan's crown! Please, where is it?"

"Hey! What's all this?" said the first soldier. "The Black Swan? And who might he be?"

"It's his crown," yelled Oliver. "It fell off his neck. You see it was his party and I had no present and so I said a poem and he got a little angry and flew away ... "

"What a lot of nonsense!" said the second soldier. "Fell off his neck! You had no present? He got angry? I'll get angry in a minute, my lad!"

"But you must give it back," said Oliver, as everyone stopped and stared. "It isn't *yours* to keep!"

"Right there for once," said the first soldier. "It belongs to the general now, and he'd do battle for that crown – pleased as Punch he is with it! You be off and tell your old Black Swan he's welcome to try any old time. We'll do battle for that crown!"

Without waiting for another word Oliver ran helter-skelter back past the Punch and Judy show and the organ-grinder, past the singing birds and the flower stalls, round the market cross and up the cobbled hill.

He must have turned at least half a dozen corners before he

realized that he could not remember the way at all. He had been so fascinated by the pedlar doll that he had scarcely noticed anything but her. He stood for a moment and looked all around, but there was nothing that he recognized.

"I do believe I'm lost," he said to himself. "Fancy losing myself just now!"

He turned again in a circle to see if he could find someone to ask the way, and found himself staring right into a familiar pair of bright eyes. Quintilian was seated on a low wall, looking very pleased with himself.

"I saw you gallop round the corner, not knowing where you were going," he said. "You seem to be in a great hurry. Why did you dash out of the shop like that? Mr Pomfret is still lost."

"Well," said Oliver, knowing what a good surprise he had. "The crown is found! Sort of, anyway – I know who has it – guess!" But before Quintilian had a chance to guess he blurted it out.

"The clockwork soldiers! Whoever they are, the smart ones in red and gold!" And Oliver breathlessly told Quintilian just what had taken place at the bric-a-brac stall.

Quintilian looked quite solemn, and thought for a moment.

"So, the crown is at the castle! That's where they live you know. Outside and up the hill. Come along, we must talk about this on the way back. Do battle for it! Fancy that. And they will you know, they will!"

"I wonder whatever happened to Mr Pomfret?" said Oliver, as they hurried on their way.

9

Where there is a Battle and the Crown is Regained

It was a very quaint and straggly little band that gathered later at the police station, and Oliver had to keep blowing his nose so that his smiles would not be seen.

The apothecary had a cake tin on his head and that slid round every time he moved. He wore a pair of large hob-nailed boots, and carried a double-barrelled musket, and he told them all that old hard lozenges were just the thing to fire at the clockwork soldiers.

"Hard as nuts," he said, "these old lozenges. Harder, in fact."

The tin soldiers were impatient to be off, and marched noisily up and down as the bugler blew one weird noise after the other, busily explaining what each noise meant to William Tell, who had brought his crossbow. He was carrying so many arrows that Oliver thought he looked more like a porcupine.

Mr Noah had a vinegar barrel round his middle, held up with tarred rope. He had brought the two camels, but was wondering whether or not the ostriches would have been a better choice.

"They can run very fast *and* kick very hard," he explained.

The proud peacock had insisted on joining them.

"To distract everybody," he said. "They are bound to stare at me!"

The acrobats had put on their most garish middles. One had a horrid dragon painted across his chest, and the other a wicked demon.

"Dragons!" one shouted.

"And demons!" shouted the other. They made fierce yelling noises, and spun round and round. The apothecary was so startled that his cake tin fell off, and he fired both barrels of his musket into the air. Quintilian had borrowed the policeman's whistle, and he blew a shrill blast. Everyone stopped short, and they formed into a straggly line.

"Attention please!" he said. "Battle they want and battle they will get! Follow me now, quick march!"

The tin soldiers insisted on marching on their own, and the bugler blew the loudest noise he had ever blown. Round the back of the police station they went as the policeman popped inside for a lantern; and nobody saw the spotted pig or the zebras or the hedgehogs (who were better now) trailing on behind. Quintilian suddenly stopped in front of a heavy wooden door in the wall. He drew back a large rusty bolt and the door swung slowly open with a groan.

"A secret route to the castle!" he said, as their eyes widened. "Mind the steps – twenty-five down and twenty-five up at the other end. Oliver, please carry the lantern!" Oliver was already carrying a sweeping brush on his shoulder, but gladly came forward to the head of the army. They all managed to count twenty-five, except the little ones behind, who had to whisper in case they were heard, and went all wrong. They finished up in a heap at the bottom of the steps and would have gone back, but of course they didn't dare without a light, and on they went, following the swaying lantern along the dark tunnel. They crept slowly onwards, pushing their way through the soft curtains of cobwebs that swung around them.

The apothecary whistled loudly inside his cake tin as the march continued through the gloom, and only stopped when it was announced by Quintilian that they were ready to start the climb out. Oliver held the lantern high, counting all the way to twenty-five. Then he stopped.

"Are you all ready?" asked Quintilian. "Oliver, you must blow out the lantern before the door is opened. Otherwise we might be seen before we are all out!"

Oliver thought he heard a noise behind them in the tunnel, but he could see nothing. The lantern was blown out, and it was inky black. The bolts were drawn back, the door opened, and fresh air blew on to their faces. Just a few more steps and they stumbled out into the moonlight.

The policeman was counting as they came through the door, and suddenly realized that there were more than he had counted at the police station.

"It's us," said the hedgehogs, with sickly little smiles.

"And us," said the zebras.

"Me too," said the spotted pig.

Mr Noah groaned.

"They can't possibly go back by themselves, and I don't see how I can leave the camels now."

"Then they must stay," said Quintilian, "but please keep behind!"

"Exactly," said one of the hedgehogs. "Just what we did."

Oliver's excitement grew and grew as he gazed straight ahead. A hill rose up across the ornamental lawns. Its base was shrouded with dark trees, and there on the top stood the castle itself, white and smooth in the moonlight.

"Not a whisper," hissed Quintilian. "There's a sentry up there on the battlements!"

Sure enough Oliver saw a tiny stiff figure move across the top of the castle. He could hear the faint stamping of his feet as he turned round and moved back.

The little army crept on tiptoe across the lawns, and reached the shelter of the trees. Quintilian ran ahead for a few yards, and then came back as Oliver relit the lantern and held it high.

"It's very muddy on the footpaths," he said. "Much too wet and slippery. Let's creep through the trees!"

Mr Noah anxiously herded his animals together behind the tin soldiers. Quintilian ordered the bugler forward and he blew an even louder noise than the one at the police station, then Oliver stepped out and shouted at the top of his voice.

"We have come to do battle for the Black Swan's crown!"

And the tin soldiers rushed up the steep slopes and out into the moonlight at the side of the castle steps. With a scream the proud peacock shot up into the nearest tree, and the acrobats wheeled round with cries of "Demons and dragons!"

Oliver lowered his sweeping brush to the ready. He could hear faint yells and bumps from the castle, and the sound of more bugling, just like theirs. Then there was a grinding noise from above as the portcullis was lifted, and the sound of doors bumping open, followed by the clatter of hooves.

With its spring whirring a large clockwork horse pranced out of the castle, a splendid figure in red, white, and gold sitting astride it. The rider's black boots shone, and his buttons winked like stars. He wore a tall hat covered in badges

and feathers, but it was to the top of even that that Oliver's eyes were drawn.

For there was the Black Swan's crown, for everyone to see! The apothecary pushed three or four lozenges down the barrels of his gun, and then a handful into his mouth as he fired the gun high into the air again.

Pair after pair of clockwork soldiers were marching swiftly out of the castle as the General galloped backwards and forwards on his horse.

"Spread out amongst the trees!" Quintilian shouted as the clockwork soldiers formed a circle right round the castle. "Get on to the muddy paths and shout as hard as you can!"

They all did as they were told, and within seconds a great chorus of shouting and jeering rang out.

"There they are!" bawled the General. "Stupid codfish standing on the paths. Up guards and after them!"

The clockwork soldiers jerked into action and spilled down from beneath the castle walls. At first they managed very well, and Quintilian was just expecting a grand retreat to start when one of them shot off his feet and careered down the muddy path like a toboggan in the snow.

Quintilian had to shout to the hedgehogs.

"Jump out of the way – mind yourselves!" They were so surprised at the sight of the sliding soldier that they were almost whisked off their feet as he disappeared into the trees, muddy from head to foot.

"That worked very well!" said Oliver. "What a good idea!"

The General was jerking backwards and forwards on his horse.

"Keep your boots clean!" he roared. "Disgraceful mess that soldier! Send him back to clean his boots!"

But there was no one able to find the clockwork soldier, because his spring had run down as he floundered in the mud.

Two or three of his comrades were shooting down the paths, to the delight of the apothecary, who peppered them with his lozenges from behind a tree. The acrobats stayed right across their path, standing gleefully on their hands as a clockwork soldier sped beneath them, and then whirred to a stop at the bottom of the hill.

"You codfish!" the General ranted and raved. "It's a trick! A dirty wicked trick! Get off those paths, and keep your boots off the mud!"

"He means keep the mud off your boots," said the spotted pig! "That's all he cares about!"

"And the crown," said Mr Noah. "He certainly cares about that!"

Mr Noah was right, for every time the General put his hands in the air to shout, he touched the crown to make quite sure that it was safe.

Meanwhile lots of the clockwork soldiers had dashed back into the castle and were just bobbing up over the battlements. All manner of strange objects came flying down into the trees as the little army crept nearer and nearer to the castle. Several cabbages and turnips whistled past their ears, and bags of flour burst on the ground, sending their white powder over both armies alike.

"Not a good idea at all," said Oliver to Quintilian, as two white clockwork soldiers chased one another round and round a tree. "Nobody will know who's who!"

The camels were dashing about in the moonlight and

scaring the clockwork soldiers from behind with loud grunts, all the time cleverly avoiding the odd things that were thrown from the walls of the castle. It seemed as though the clockwork soldiers were now running short of ammunition, for they had resorted to throwing their feather pillows, which floated down gently, trailing clouds of white feathers in the air.

The General was almost beside himself with rage.

"Come back out here!" he cried, shaking a fist at the battlements as a pillow burst on a spike of the crown and covered him with feathers.

"It's just a bunch of donkeys and children! You shall all live for a week on iron rations! Bring out the cannon!"

The zebras tugged anxiously at Mr Noah's sleeve at the mention of the cannon, but Quintilian laughed scornfully.

"That old thing! It shoots potatoes – sometimes, that is, when it shoots at all! And they don't seem to have any real idea where we are."

Slowly the things stopped floating down from the castle, and then, to the sound of a bugle, a very large shiny brass cannon was trundled out under the portcullis, followed by two or three clockwork soldiers dragging sacks of potatoes.

The proud peacock screamed and spread out his gorgeous tail from the treetop. The clockwork soldiers looked amazed, and began to turn the cannon round that way as the General rode back and forth on his horse.

"Get that pigeon!" he yelled. "Show that bird a thing or two!"

The proud peacock screamed with rage at being called a pigeon, and spread out his tail wider and wider, contemptuous of the clockwork soldiers and their cannon.

Then Oliver saw something very strange. One of the clockwork soldiers behind the brass cannon was standing very still, right in the middle of reaching for a handful of potatoes. And up on the battlements several more of them were leaning about in very odd positions.

"Whatever does it mean?" he asked Quintilian. "Lots of the clockwork soldiers seem to have stopped!"

Quintilian looked around quickly, and then jumped up and down, and wagged his tail with excitement.

"Of course!" he barked. "They are all running down–they dashed out in the middle of the night without getting wound up properly!"

The General seemed quite unable to understand what was happening, and was waving his sword high in the air, shouting "Fire! Fire!" as the proud peacock turned slowly back and forth in the pale moonlight, without showing the least concern.

As Oliver watched, scarcely able to think what might happen next, there was a rush of movement up in the castle, followed by the loud blowing of a bugle. The clockwork soldiers' flag was being lowered from the pole, and the tin soldiers from the little army appeared gleefully over the battlements.

Quintilian jumped forward and called out at the top of his voice.

"The castle is taken! The clockwork soldiers have all stopped! Only the General is left–after him! After him!"

With the crown shining brightly the General jerked off the hilltop and plunged down the pathway into the trees, with the whole pack behind him whooping and cheering.

"Codfish!" he roared. "Stupid codfish! I'll have you all for my breakfast!"

For a moment it looked as though he might escape, as no one could match the speed of his dappled horse. And then it started to happen to him.

First of all the horse began to slow down, little by little, and then the General himself stopped waving his arms so wildly and slowly tilted backwards in his saddle. As his head rocked he lifted both hands up anxiously to steady the wobbling crown as the whole little army closed in with the greatest excitement, cheered on by the proud peacock.

As they surrounded the General his last jerky movements were coming to a halt, and his dappled horse shot out two legs forwards, and two behind, with an anxious whirring of the key underneath his saddle.

Again the Crown toppled, and slid backwards, but somehow it stayed on top of the General's hat as eager hands rose all around to catch it. With one last shudder and click the General and his horse stood quite still.

Oliver jumped up and down snatching at the air.

"I do believe it's out of reach," he said at last. "What can we do?"

Without a moment of hesitation William Tell stepped up from the little army that crowded round the General.

"This will be the proudest moment of my life," he said, as he reached over his shoulder for an arrow.

"Nothing but apples for all these years, and now a golden crown!" Quintilian moved everybody into a half-circle around the General as William Tell took careful aim.

"Years and years of practice will not have been in vain,"

said Quintilian, as Oliver edged forward with a triumphant smile.

Twang! The arrow sped from the bow. With a loud ringing noise it struck the crown right in the middle, and tumbled it into Oliver's snatching hands!

Cheer upon cheer rang out, and William Tell was almost beside himself with pride. The tin soldiers fired a salute of potatoes from the brass cannon, and the policeman appeared from nowhere, counting one and all.

"Only the hedgehogs missing," he said, as Oliver lifted the crown high above his head.

"I see them!" called the peacock. "Fast asleep on one of those feather pillows!"

Mr Noah went off to awaken them as the tin soldiers marched proudly down from the castle with the bugler at their head.

Five minutes later the door banged shut in the moonlight, and the victorious little army counted down the twenty-five steps into the tunnel.

"Everyone seems to be covered in mud!" said Quintilian.

"And feathers," shouted one acrobat.

"And flour!" shouted the other.

"My lozenges were just the thing," said the apothecary.

"And me!" said the proud peacock. "I was just the one to catch their attention!"

"I caught the crown," said Oliver, watching it shine in the light of the lantern.

"I shot it down!" said William Tell. "Easy as pie!"

The triumphant procession climbed up the steps at the other end of the tunnel and burst out into the cobbled street. With Oliver at the head holding the crown they marched on through the gathering crowd. The goose came out of her house quacking delightedly as windows and doors opened all along the route to the archway.

In spite of the great noise the Black Swan was quite still, his head folded gracefully beneath his great dark wings.

"Brooding about his crown I should think," said Quintilian. "Fetch a ladder from the fire establishment! This should make everything all right again!"

Within a few moments the policeman and the apothecary came back with a long red ladder and leaned it against the pedestal. Oliver climbed halfway up the ladder and then leaned down and took the crown from the policeman. With great care he continued his climb. Reaching the top he coughed respectfully, and tapped gently on the great bird's wing. Before a word could be spoken Oliver slid the crown over his head and down the silken neck, until it nestled in the Black Swan's breast.

"Once this fell out of the skies!" recited Oliver proudly.

"What a marvellous surprise!" murmured the Black Swan.

Everyone sighed with relief at his obvious pleasure.

"Now back around your neck it lies!" they all chorused.

After a few moments of watching, in which the Black Swan seemed quite unable to speak another word, Quintilian turned to the crowd.

"There was a great battle", he said, "and the crown has been won. Everything is as it should be again!"

They all trooped away down the cobbled street as the Black Swan bent his neck again and again, turning the sparkling crown slowly in the soft light.

Epilogue

THE following day Oliver could not resist joining the visitors to the museum. They all agreed that they had never seen a more handsome bird than the Black Swan, nor a finer crown.

After a few thoughts about the great battle Oliver hurried around the corner and stood before the silent little figure of the tobacco boy. There was nothing at all in his little black box, and Oliver knew that all was back to normal for the time being. Sure enough Mr Pomfret was there at his table with the zebras in front of him, and a paintbrush in his hand. Oliver could not get too near for all the people, but he was sure that he could still see traces of mud on the zebra's hooves.

The acrobats were motionless beside their handsome box, having changed the dragon and the demon for polka-dots, and the tin soldiers were standing stiffly to attention.

Looking remarkably smart, thought Oliver. Considering what happened last night!

Oliver wished that he could find the pedlar doll so that he could thank her, but she was not to be found.

She must be somewhere with her perfumes and ribbons, he thought. What a good idea it was to go to the market. I hope that she has heard the good news!

Turning round the last corner towards the locksmith's shop Oliver wondered what everyone would think if he went through the door and turned that tiny key ...

A tall thin man who reminded him of the General was

standing at the window. He was not looking at the little pot dog at that moment but running his gaze over the cluttered shelves. As Oliver approached the man turned to him.

"Nothing much in here to interest children," he said. "Nothing but locks and keys."

Oliver could see Quintilian's eyes gleaming over the top of the thin man's hat. He half stopped and nodded shyly.

"No, nothing but locks and keys," he repeated.

Then, glancing up again, he thought he caught the wink in Quintilian's eye.

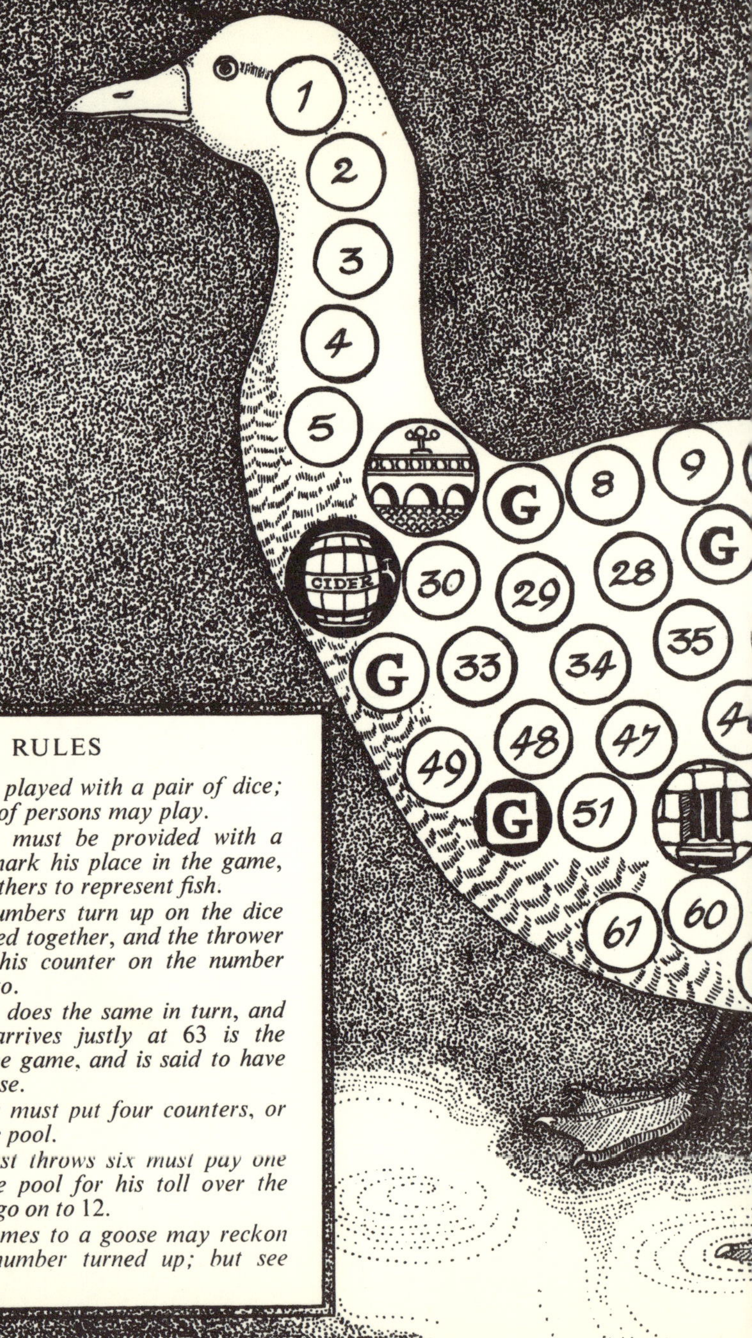

RULES

1. *The game is played with a pair of dice; any number of persons may play.*
2. *Each player must be provided with a counter to mark his place in the game, and twelve others to represent fish.*
3. *Whatever numbers turn up on the dice must be added together, and the thrower must place his counter on the number they add up to.*
4. *Each player does the same in turn, and whosoever arrives justly at 63 is the winner of the game, and is said to have won the Goose.*
5. *Each player must put four counters, or fish, into the pool.*
6. *Whoever first throws six must pay one fish into the pool for his toll over the bridge, and go on to 12.*
7. *Whoever comes to a goose may reckon twice the number turned up; but see rule 15.*